Littlebury Tunnel

INTRODUCTORY

Why yet another book on railways? And why, in particular, on Quakers and railways? The short answer is that Quakers provide a cross-section of people involved in railways – engineers and station masters, directors and engine drivers – and that I am interested in people and railways. My father would talk to me of the effect upon the railway scene of individual friendships and enmities, partnerships and rivalries, and of the ways in which vaulting ambition could lead to ill-considered and grandiose schemes and in which timidity or entrenched prejudice could delay necessary reform.

By concentrating on the small Quaker community I have hoped to depict a microcosm of the railway world of people and some of the effects their thinking had on each other, for British Quakerdom in the 19th century was a small body, allowing a fairly ready study of who was related to, or at school with, whom; of who corresponded with and influenced whom, so that railways can be seen in terms of personal relationships.

This booklet is restricted to England: I have not attempted to cover the minimal Quaker involvement in Wales or Scotland, or the larger involvement in Ireland, or the considerable enterprise of British and Irish Quakers overseas. The story of Quakers and railways is episodic rather than a logically developing story and the arrangement of this booklet reflects that fact. If the number of portraits seems disproportionate I do not apologise: it is a deliberate decision — for, though the portrait can on occasion lead us astray, it helps us more often than not to understand the person more fully.

I am grateful for an upbringing as ecumenical in relation to railways as to religion. I was born in 1922, neatly sandwiched between the royal assent to the Railways Act 1921 and its operative date of 1 January 1923. The pre-grouping traditions lived on. I spent my infancy in London & North Western territory, my childhood in that of the South Eastern & Chatham and my adolescence on the Great Western. I went to the Quaker School at Ackworth, travelling either by Great Northern from Kings Cross or by Great Western to Banbury and thence by Great Central through Woodford & Hinton, Rugby, Nottingham and Sheffield. Ackworth itself was on a stretch of Midland & North Eastern Joint and not far off was the Lancashire & Yorkshire at Featherstone and the slumbering Hull & Barnsley at Upton & North Elmsall or Kirk Smeaton.

These July 1936 photographs show the Ackworth end-of-term loading of trunks, which will trundle down to the station for dispatch 'Luggage in advance'. And, having sent our luggage, let us start our own journey through the book.

Edward H Milligan (signature)

Edward H. Milligan

1

THE QUAKER BACKGROUND

This painting, 'A monthly meeting at Earith 1836' by Samuel Lucas (1805-1870) of Hitchin, depicts a deputation from the Yearly Meeting of British Quakers to the area business meeting of Friends in Huntingdonshire. Quaker church government was neither congregational nor hierarchical. The principal meeting for business was the area monthly meeting; several of these formed the regional quarterly meeting; and the quarterly meetings in Britain formed the Yearly Meeting, a separate Yearly Meeting being established in Ireland.

There were some 20,000 Quakers in Britain in 1800, the numbers falling to just over 13,000 in 1860 and rising to 17,000 in 1900. It was a small and tightly-knit community, though not quite as dynastic and ingrown as is sometimes asserted, as there was a steady stream of those joining by convincement. The widening circles of meetings for church affairs served to knit the community together: they were also perhaps responsible for the complexities of inter-marriage between Quaker clans.

The Society was also bound together by the visits of Friends 'travelling in the ministry'. Out of the silent expectant waiting upon God characteristic of Quaker worship, the ministry of the word might be given to any worshipper, women as much as men. It was recognised, however, that to some the gift was especially entrusted: these Friends were known as recorded ministers, a practice now discontinued in Britain. It was never a separated, much less a paid, ministry, and the husband or wife of a minister would look after the business and family if their partner felt called to travel in the British Isles or overseas.

The monthly and quarterly meetings were social occasions as well as meetings for business, often involving an overnight stay. The hospitality of a Quaker home might bring together a farmer and an ironmaster, a pharmacist and a woollen merchant, and the conversation, in which strong-minded women Friends would take as much part as men, might well resemble what we would now call a interdisciplinary seminar. From conversations like these new ideas grew.

Links were also forged between those who had shared together a Quaker 'guarded education'. It was not until 1871 that the abolition of religious tests enabled non-conformists to enter Oxford or Cambridge. The youthful energy, intellectual curiosity and practical abilities which young Quakers would otherwise have put into academic studies were channelled into industry and commerce, while their interests in natural history and in pure and applied science kept their minds supple. Quakers had a natural tendency to question received ideas – and their innate caution was matched by a sometimes ruthless pursuit of first principles.

FROM WAGGON WAY TO RAILWAY

As coal mining developed in the late 16th and early 17th centuries there were increasing transport problems getting the coal to the nearest river for shipment. Waggon ways began to be laid in Northumberland and County Durham from the early 17th century, simple tracks of wooden planks on which small trucks could run, either pushed by boys or drawn by horses. Gradually the use of such waggon ways became more general and more sophisticated.

About 1740 the Quaker ironmaster Abraham Darby II (1711-1763) fitted his Coalbrookdale waggons with cast iron wheels with an inner flange and cast iron axle-trees, and in 1767 Richard Reynolds (1735-1816), manager of the works (whose portrait is shown here), replaced the wooden rails by cast iron ones. Abraham Darby II's widow, Abiah, writing about 1775, describes the development under her husband and Reynolds:

'They used to carry their coal upon horses' backs, but he got roads made and laid with Sleepers and rails, as they have them in the North of England. And one waggon with three horses will bring as much as 20 horses used to bring on horses' backs. But this laying the road with wood begot a scarcity and raised the price of it, so that of late years the laying of the rails of Cast Iron was substituted; which altho expensive answers well for wear and duration. We have in the different works near 20 miles of this road, which costs upwards of £800 a mile.'

River transport also presented problems. The Severn barges were pulled by men who often had to scramble along the precipitous and rocky banks of the river, and in 1772 Richard Reynolds pressed for legislation for a towpath. Though he was unsuccessful, his son William

(1758-1803) demonstrated the possibilities by himself making a 2-mile towpath from Coalport to the Iron Bridge. He was also the moving spirit and substantially the designer of the 'upper canal' and the 1788 inclined plane (still to be seen) which connected it by a drop of 73 feet to the 'lower canal' level with the Ketley ironworks.

Telford commented: 'A double railway being laid upon the inclined plane, the loaded boat in passing down brought up another boat containing a load nearly equal to one-third part of that which passed down. The velocities of the boats were regulated by a brake acting upon a large wheel placed upon the axis on which the ropes connected with the carriage were coiled.'

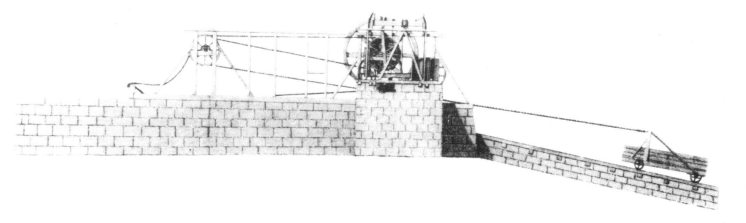

1825 STOCKTON & DARLINGTON

The Stockton & Darlington was opened on 27 September 1825. But it was as early as 18 September 1810, when the 'New Cut' was opened, reducing the journey time on the lower Tees and making Stockton a deep sea port, that the Quaker Benjamin Flounders (1768-1846) of Yarm, better known to Quakers for the educational trust that bears his name, seconded a resolution for appointing a committee to see how practicable it would be to build a railway or canal from the Durham coalfields to Stockton. Three years later costs had escalated and the project was dropped.

On 4 September 1818 Edward Pease (1767-1858), a Darlington Quaker and coalowner whose portrait is shown here, convened a meeting attended by his 19-year-old son Joseph, by Benjamin Flounders and by such other Quakers as John Grimshaw of Bishopwearmouth, Thomas Richardson and the prominent Darlington banker Jonathan Backhouse. As a result, and after two parliamentary bills had come to nought, the Stockton & Darlington Railway Act received the royal assent on 21 April 1821.

At the same time Edward Pease and George Stephenson (1781-1848) met. Stephenson, though impoverished in his youth, was now comfortably off and much sought after as an engineer, so that Pease was fortunate in securing him for the Stockton & Darlington.

It was Stephenson who persuaded Pease to think in terms of steam rather than horses for haulage though, since the first purpose of the railway was rapid transit of coal, passenger trains were horse-drawn until 1833.

A select party made a trial trip on the railway the day before the official 1825 opening, Pease and his sons among them. But they could not share in the opening celebrations, for Edward's 20-year-old son Issac had died during the previous night and Henry, the youngest of the children, felt acutely all his long life 'the mixture that attends all earthly things' as he recalled 'this day of victory and rejoicing, and sore sorrow and bereavement'.

For the Stockton & Darlington's 1875 jubilee Jonathan Backhouse's irrepressible great-grandson Samuel Tuke Richardson (b 1846) produced an album of cartoons, one of which, 'Arrival of No. 1 Engine at Aycliffe', is reproduced here.

Joseph Pease (1799-1872), second of Edward's children, took the next step – the development of Middlesbrough. In 1828 parliamentary authority was obtained for a Stockton & Middlesbrough branch to the railway, the intended terminus being but a farm house with one or two labourers' dwellings and a few trees. On this site the future port was developed. In 1833 Joseph became the first Quaker to enter parliament and the railway interests in the family now rested on Henry (1807-1881), whose portrait is shown here. In his later years he would recall that he was the very last of the pre-opening party of 1825 who could say they were the very first people to travel by the aid of steam.

His railway interests led in 1838 to the Bishop Auckland & Weardale, in 1846 to the Middlesbrough & Redcar. It was, however, the traversing of the Pennines that continued to exercise Henry's mind and imagination and on 20 July 1854 he cut the second sod of the the Darlington & Barnard Castle.

Earlier that year he had, with Joseph Sturge (whom we shall shortly meet) and Robert Charleton, made on behalf of British Quakers the hazardous journey to Petersburg to speak to the Czar of Russia in the hope of averting the Crimean War, a journey which led to calumny in the popular press:

Joseph Sturge
Went over to urge
Peace on the Emperor Nicholas:
Henry Pease
Crossed over the seas
On the same errand ridiculous.

In summer 1856 the Barnard Castle line was opened and Henry Pease immediately began to plan a line over Stainmoor to join the London & North Western at Tebay. Stainmoor summit was 1374 feet and the engineering the line demanded was formidable – but it proved uniformly prosperous, conveying coke and coal westbound to Barrow-in-Furness and iron ore eastbound in return.

In 1863, when the Stockton & Darlington was incorporated into the North Eastern, it had some 185 route miles, extending from Redcar, Saltburn and Guisborough in the east to Tebay and Penrith in the west and Frosterley and Consett in the north-west.

STOCKTON & DARLINGTON
RAILWAY
COACHES.

The **SUMMER ARRANGEMENTS** will cease on the 30th Instant, and the Trains run the same as last season until further notice: *viz.*—

Winter Arrangements, commencing October 1st, 1840.

ST. HELEN'S AUCKLAND TO DARLINGTON.		DARLINGTON TO ST. HELEN'S AUCKLAND.	
First Trip	at half-past Eight o'Clock.	First Trip	at half-past Eight o'Clock.
Second Trip	at One "	Second Trip	at One "
Third Trip	at Five "	Third Trip	at Five "

DARLINGTON TO STOCKTON.		STOCKTON TO DARLINGTON.	
Merchandize Train	at half-past Six o'Clock.	First Class Train	at 10 min. bef. Eight o'Clock
First Class Train	at half-past Nine "	Merchandize Train at 10 min. bef. Nine	
Merchandize Train	at Eleven "	First Class Train	at 20 min. past Twelve "
First Class Train	at Two "	Merchandize Train at 20 min. past Two	
Merchandize Train	at Four "	First Class Train	at 20 min. past Four "
First Class Train	at Six "	Merchandize Train at 20 min. past Six	

STOCKTON TO MIDDLESBRO'.			MIDDLESBRO' TO STOCKTON		
First	Trip	at Eight o'Clock.	*First	Trip	at half-past Seven o'Clock.
Second	do	at Nine "	Second	do	at half-past Eight "
*Third	do	at Ten "	Third	do	at half-past Nine "
Fourth	do	at Eleven "	Fourth	do	at half-past Ten "
Fifth	do	at half-past Twelve "	*Fifth	do	at Twelve "
Sixth	do	at half-past One "	Sixth	do	at One "
*Seventh	do	at half-past Two "	Seventh	do	at Two "
Eighth	do	at half-past Three "	Eighth	do	at Three "
Ninth	do	at half-past Four "	*Ninth	do	at Four "
Tenth	do	at half-past Five "	Tenth	do	at Five "
*Eleventh	do	at a quarter bef. Seven "	Eleventh	do	at Six "

* Are in connexion with the first class Trains to and from Darlington.

Tickets must be taken at least **Five** Minutes before the Trains start.

NO SMOKING ALLOWED IN ANY OF THE COMPANY'S COACHES.

MARKET COACHES.

A Coach and Cattle Carriage will leave St. Helen's Auckland, on **Mondays**, at half-past **Six** o'Clock; and **Shildon**, at **Seven** in the **Morning**.

HORSES, CATTLE, AND CARRIAGES, CAREFULLY CONVEYED BETWEEN STOCKTON AND DARLINGTON, BY THE MERCHANDIZE TRAINS.

Horse, 2s.—Gig, 2s. or Horse and Gig, 3s.—Four-wheeled Carriage, 5s., or with Two Horses, 8s.—Horned Cattle, 1s. 6d. each.—Sheep, 4d. each, or 5s. per Score.—Dogs, 1s. each

If by the FIRST-CLASS Train— Horse 3s.—Gig, 3s.—Horse and Gig, 4s.—Four-wheeled Carriage, 5s., or with Two Horses, 9s.

Railway Office, Darlington, September 25th, 1840.

COATES AND FARMER, PRINTERS, HIGH ROW, DARLINGTON.

1830 LIVERPOOL & MANCHESTER

During the first quarter of the 19th century Manchester's population grew from 100,000 to 150,000 and Liverpool's from 60,000 to 135,000. This vast growth of population (and trade) was reflected in the Quaker world by the 1818 division of Hardshaw Monthly Meeting, the area business meeting for south Lancashire, into Hardshaw East and Hardshaw West, mysterious cognomens which persist to this day.

Proposals for a waggon way between the two towns had been made from the beginning of the century: it was 30 miles between them and canal journeys varied between 43 miles (Mersey & Irwell) and 58 miles (Leeds & Liverpool, in which many Quakers had been involved). Moreover, the canal monopoly was increasingly irksome to merchants, who in 1821 formed a provisional committee to explore the possibility of a railway. Early in 1824 some of them went to see George Stephenson's work on the Stockton & Darlington and by that June he had moved to Liverpool and begun a survey.

Among the merchants was the Quaker James Cropper (1773-1840) whose portrait is shown here. He was very wealthy, a notable philanthropist (active in the anti-slavery movement and in promoting agricultural improvement) but perhaps inclined to be opinionated and certainly on occasion abrasive, so that he was to George Stephenson and his son Robert a continuing thorn in the flesh ('Now George, thou must get on with the railway and have it finished without further delay').

Cropper had opposed locomotives and favoured stationary engines with pulley-ropes. The Rainhill Trials of 6 to 14 October 1829 left no doubt that the locomotive had come to stay and on Wednesday 15 September 1830 the Liverpool & Manchester was officially opened. Tragedy, as we know, marred that day when the MP William Huskisson was fatally injured.

A series of 1832 engravings is among the early efforts to popularise railways: the one shown here, of Olive Mount Cutting, Liverpool, perhaps re-echoes something of the interaction of the romantic movement and intermediate technology.

The Liverpool & Manchester was, unlike the Stockton & Darlington, conceived from the outset as for both passengers and freight. Regular passenger services began on Friday 17 September 1830 but on the previous day some 130 passengers were carried on special trains between the two towns, many if not most being Quakers attending Lancashire Quarterly Meeting which was held in normal course at Liverpool that day.

It is sometimes claimed that George Bradshaw issued his first timetable in 1839 in the teeth of opposition from railway companies. It is perhaps useful to be reminded that there were at least departure sheets before Bradshaw. The one shown here was in the possession of Thomas Robson (1768-1852) who had settled with his family in Liverpool in 1822: his wife Elizabeth (1771-1843) was a recorded minister in the Society of Friends and indefatigible in her travels. Railways were to change the leisured pattern of the travels of ministering Friends as well as that of meetings for church affairs.

Railways designed for passengers demand coaches and Thomas Clarke Worsdell (1788-1862) was early on the scene. In stage coach days he had been apprenticed to a coachbuilder in Long Acre, London, but between 1812 and 1816 he moved to Lancashire where he was in business as a coachmaker and where he and his wife joined Friends. In 1827 the family settled in Liverpool and the following year he and his son Nathaniel (1809-1886) were invited to tea by Stephenson to discuss drawings of a coach for the Liverpool & Manchester. He was soon appointed superintendent of coaching for the railway and he and Nathaniel worked together until 1837, Stephenson later describing TCW as 'the best coachbuilder I ever knew'.

Replicas of Worsdell coaches were made for the 1930 Liverpool & Manchester centenary and that shown here is now in the National Railway Museum at York.

As for the Worsdell family, no less than three generations were notable in railway history, as we shall find in later pages.

1832
TOWARDS THE MIDLAND

The first railway in the midlands owed its origin, like the Stockton & Darlington, to the need to transport coal. With the development of the north-west Leicestershire coalfields the need became urgent and in October 1828 William Stinson, a partner in Whitwick Colliery, near Coalville, went to see the Stockton & Darlington and, on returning, wrote to the 40-year-old Quaker John Ellis (1789-1862) of Beaumont Leys to arouse his interest. Ellis, a farmer and anti-slavery figure, was a friend of James Cropper who sent him post-haste to see George Stephenson, then at work on the Liverpool & Manchester. His son Robert was appointed engineer and on 17 July 1832 the Leicester & Swannington was opened.

John Ellis's Journal for 1 January 1833: 'Went up to the Railway this day with John Sturge and Captain Moorsom RN, their object being to see how the smoke and steam of Locomotive Engines would operate on passengers in the Tunnel. They were delighted with the experiment we tried by taking "The Phoenix" through a few minutes after "The Comet". Met George Stephenson at Bagworth. All three came to dine. They are all interesting men. Captain Moorsom commanded the "Fury" in the battle of Algiers'.

John Sturge, a Birmingham corn-merchant, was one of the first directors of the London & Birmingham, which was incorporated 6 May 1833, the line being opened in part in 1837 and fully the next year. Sturge's brother Joseph (1793-1859), whose portrait is shown here, also joined the London & Birmingham board. Joseph Sturge's first wife was daughter to James Cropper and Cropper's son Edward was also on the London & Birmingham board.

Rail links quickly spread. In August 1839 the Birmingham & Derby Junction was opened, connecting Derby with the London & Birmingham at Hampton-in-Arden, thus providing a rail connection from the east midlands to London. 1842 saw the direct line from Whitacre through Water Orton to Birmingham. In June 1839 the Midland Counties had opened from Nottingham to Derby and in summer 1840 from near Long Eaton (midway between the towns) south to Leicester and thence to join the London & Birmingham at Rugby, thus outmanoeuvering the Birmingham & Derby Junction.

That same summer of 1840 the North Midland opened from Derby through Masborough to Leeds, the Leeds & Selby and the York & North Midland between

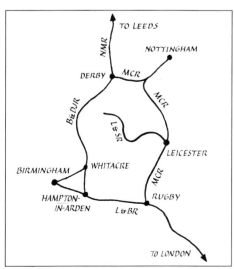

them completing a rail connection from London to York. Another 12 years were to pass before the East Coast Main Line reached Doncaster direct. In 1841, as this Bradshaw shows, one could leave York at 8.45 in the morning and be in London within 12 hours – a magnificent achievement compared with 20 hours in a stage coach. The next year the best train was down to 10 hours 15 minutes.

In 1844 the Midland Counties, Birmingham & Derby Junction and North Midland amalgamated to become the Midland – a company to remain until the regrouping of 1923. John Ellis became deputy chairman and moved into Belgrave, Leicester. The chairman, George Hudson

MIDLAND COUNTIES RAILWAY.

Fares.—Nottingham to Leicester 6s. and 4s. 6d., Derby to Leicester 6s. and 5s., Nottingham to Loughboro' 3s. 6d. and 2s. 6d. Derby to Loughboro' 3s. 6d. and 3s., Leicester to Loughboro' 2s. 6d. and 2s.—* To these trains 3rd class carriages will be attached.

Mls.	STATIONS. Departure from	DOWN TRAINS. a. m.	a. m.	a. m.	a. m.	p. m.	Mail p. m.	Sundays. a. m.	a. m.	p. m.	Mail p. m.
	London	..	6 0	9 15	*11 0	5 0	8 30	..	8 0	..	8 30
	Birmingham	..	8 30	..	1 15	5 30	..	..	..	..	..
	Rugby	..	9 50	12 50	2 45	8 50	12 40	..	12 15	..	12 40
7¾	Ullesthorpe	..	10 12	1 10	3 10	9 10	1 4	..	12 35	..	1 4
11	Broughton Astley	..	10 20	..	3 20	..	..	..	..	..	..
16½	Wigston	..	10 33	..	3 33	..	..	..	..	..	..
20	Leicester	*7 45	10 50	1 45	3 50	9 45	1 44	7 45	1 10	6 30	1 44
24¾	Syston	8 0	11 3	1 58	4 5	9 58	1 59	8 0	1 25	6 43	1 59
27¾	Sileby	8 9	11 14	..	4 15	..	..	8 9	..	6 52	..
30	Barrow	8 17	..	..	4 25	..	..	8 17	..	7 0	..
32½	Loughborough	8 25	11 30	2 18	4 35	10 18	2 23	8 25	1 45	7 8	2 23
37¼	Kegworth	8 37	11 42	2 30	4 50	10 30	..	8 37	2 0	7 20	..
41½	Long-Eaton	9 0	..	..	5 10	..	..	9 0	..	7 36	..
44½	Beeston	9 8	..	..	5 20	..	..	9 8	..	7 45	..
47½	Nottingham, arr. at	9 15	12 15	3 0	5 30	11 0	3 9	9 15	2 30	8 0	3 9
42¼	Sawley, arrival at	8 55	..	..	5 10	..	..	8 55	..	7 10	..
45¼	Borrowash ,, ,,	9 5	..	..	5 20	..	..	9 5	..	7 50	..
49¼	Derby ,, ,,	9 15	12 15	3 0	5 30	11 0	3 9	9 15	2 30	8 0	3 9
	Sheffield ,, ,,	11 45	..	5 15	8 15	..	5 47	..	5 15	..	5 47
	Leeds ,, ,,	1 30	..	6 45	10 0	..	7 8	..	7 0	..	7 8
	York ,, ,,	2 15	..	7 30	..	..	7 42	..	7 45	..	7 42
	Hull ,, ,,	..	..	..	..	..	9 30	..	..	..	9 30

	STATIONS. Departure fr.	UP TRAINS. a. m.	* a. m.	a. m.	p. m.	p. m.	Mail p. m.	Sundays. a. m.	a. m.	p. m.	Mail p. m.
	Hull	..	..	*6 45	9 30	*2 0	4 45	..	..	..	4 45
	York	..	..	8 45	11 0	4 0	6 0	..	7 0	..	6 0
	Leeds	..	6 0	9 30	11 45	4 15	6 40	..	7 45	..	6 40
	Sheffield	..	7 30	10 45	1 15	5 30	8 0	..	9 15	..	8 0
	Derby	*8 15	10 30	1 15	4 15	8 0	10 40	6 45	12 15	6 30	10 40
4	Borrowash	..	..	..	..	8 10	..	6 56	..	6 40	..
7	Sawley	..	..	..	..	8 20	..	7 5	..	6 50	..
	Nottingham	8 15	10 30	1 15	4 15	8 0	10 40	6 45	12 15	6 30	10 40
3	Beeston	8 23	..	..	..	8 8	..	6 51	..	6 40	..
6	Long-Eaton	8 30	..	..	..	8 16	..	7 0	..	6 50	..
12	Kegworth	8 50	11 3	1 48	4 40	8 35	..	7 25	12 45	7 5	..
16¾	Loughborough	9 5	11 15	2 0	4 52	8 50	11 28	7 39	1 0	7 20	11 28
19¼	Barrow	9 15	..	..	5 0	8 58	..	7 49	..	7 28	..
21¾	Sileby	9 24	..	..	5 8	9 8	..	7 55	..	7 38	..
24½	Syston	9 33	11 35	2 20	5 15	9 15	11 52	8 5	1 20	7 45	11 52
29¼	Leicester	9 50	11 55	2 40	5 30	9 30	12 10	8 30	1 40	8 0	12 10
32¾	Wigston	10 0	..	..	5 40	..	..	8 40	..	..	..
38¼	Broughton Astley	10 15	..	..	5 55	..	..	8 58	..	..	..
41½	Ullesthorpe	10 25	12 20	3 15	6 10	..	12 47	9 10	2 15	..	12 47
49¼	Rugby, arrival at	11 0	12 45	*3 40	6 35	..	1 8	9 30	2 40	..	1 8
	Birmingham ,,	1 45	2 15	7 45	10 30	..	..	..	..	..	..
	London ,, ,,	3 30	5 30	8 15	11 15	..	5 30	1 30	7 15	..	5 30

(1800-1871), was colourful, visionary but too often unscrupulous; but his downfall in 1849 brought few problems for the Midland, for as a later historian said:

> ...although there were suggestions that he was not at all times quite loyal to their interests, it must be stated that the committee of investigation on the Midland found that the accounts had been faithfully kept, and that a strong and powerful directorate had preserved the honour and reputation of the Company unsullied. That this was so, a large measure of praise is due to Mr John Ellis, the hard-headed Quaker, who subsequently undertook the controlling influence.

John Ellis now became chairman, serving until 1858 and holding office long enough to see the Midland's 1857 extension from Leicester southwards to Bedford and Hitchin, giving it by courtesy of the Great Northern a route to London. The Great Northern's courtesy was less than it might have been, necessitating the later line from Bedford to St Pancras – but that is another story.

Ellis, whose portrait is shown here, was MP for Leicester 1848-52, a town councillor and magistrate, but refused the mayoralty on account of 'objections he entertained as a member of the Society of Friends'.

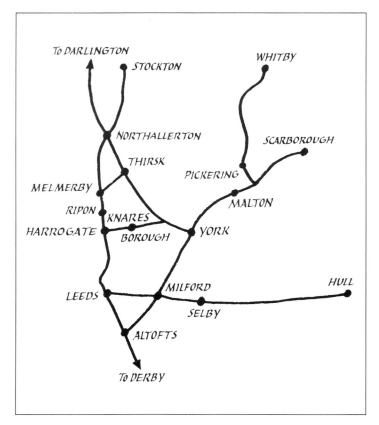

1834 TOWARDS THE NORTH EASTERN

The development of railways in the north-east was complex. We have already looked at the Stockton & Darlington: we must now turn to Yorkshire.

The Leeds & Selby (1834) was first in the field, an isolated stretch of line until 1839 when George Hudson's York & North Midland was opened from York to meet it at Milford, the line extending next year to join the new Derby to Leeds railway at Altofts, near Normanton. The Hull & Selby also dates from 1840. In 1845 the York & North Midland began services from York to Scarborough, with a branch to Pickering, and at the same time bought the 1835-6 Whitby & Pickering.

Another Hudson company began services from York to Darlington in 1841. Other companies continued northward to Newcastle (1844) and Berwick (1847): their 1847 amalgamation as the York Newcastle & Berwick consolidated Hudson's empire, for he had already acquired for the York & North Midland both the Leeds & Selby and the Hull & Selby.

We must now turn to Henry Tennant (1823-1910), son of a Quaker farmer at Countersett, north Yorkshire: the meeting house where he worshipped is shown here. After schooldays at Ackworth he started his railway career in 1844 on the Brandling Junction, which linked Gateshead, South Shields and Monkwearmouth.

In 1846 Tennant joined the Leeds & Thirsk, a non-Hudson company incorporated the previous year. The line was partly opened in 1848 and fully the following year, and became in 1851 the Leeds Northern. When in 1852 it extended from Melmerby through Northallerton to Stockton, the former Hudson companies (he himself had been discreditied in 1849) felt their territories threatened. On the other hand a Hudson-operated company had opened from York to Knaresborough in 1848 and, taken over by the York & North Midland and extended to Harrogate in 1851, was seen as invading Leeds Northern territory.

Competition was leading to administrative and financial chaos. It was due in no small measure to Tennant that in 1854 the Leeds Northern, York & North Midland and York Newcastle & Berwick came together as the North Eastern with more than 720 route miles to its credit – more than any other company at that time. And in 1863 it took over the Stockton & Darlington.

Joseph Rowntree I (1801–1859), a grocer in Pavement, York, whose portrait is shown above, proposed a motion at an 1835 public meeting in favour of a railway – 4 years later it became the York & North Midland. In 1849 he was, in his absence, appointed a director when, due to the Hudson crisis, 'its affairs were in a deplorable condition'. He accepted appointment reluctantly and worked assiduously for 6 months but at the ensuing shareholders' meeting resigned 'from a difference of opinion between himself and the Shareholders' Investigation Committee'.

Newman Cash (1792–1866), a Leeds stuff merchant, had been among the original promoters of the Leeds & Selby and was a director of the Leeds Northern, continuing with the North Eastern until his death. His father had settled in Coventry as a stuff manufacturer, establishing the business later to become Cash's of name tape fame.

Newman Cash, Samuel Priestman and Joseph Rowntree were all founder directors of the Friends Provident Institution, established in 1832 with its offices in Bradford.

Henry Tennant (whose portrait is shown right) was accountant to the North Eastern 1854-71, general manager 1871-91 and a director 1891-1910. His negotiations were not without toughness: he relished the remark made of him, 'If you want a good fighting man, commend me to a Quaker'. If he was as firm as steel on any question of principle, he was nevertheless essentially a pacificator and conciliator. His was a familiar figure in the parliamentary committee room, always certain of his facts and of his case. Under cross-examination he was 'as cool as an algebraic problem' and he possessed 'an uncommon gift of reticence, which he frequently employed to the discomfiture of his interrogators'. He never took anything for granted and he always verified every statement before he made it.

Samuel Priestman (1800–1872), whose portrait is shown above, had been a miller at Holbeck, Leeds, and then at Kirkstall. At 40 he retired, being in indifferent health, and in 1844 settled at East Mount, Hull. It was no inactive retirement. Amongst many other tasks he became in 1850 a director of the York & North Midland, continuing with the North Eastern until his death. His first wife, who died in 1837, was first cousin to Joseph Rowntree and his younger sister had married one of Joseph's brothers, while another sister had married a brother of John Ellis of the Midland. His journal, now in the Public Record Office, illustrates the day to day problems of railway management.

1840
BIRMINGHAM & GLOUCESTER

The Birmingham & Gloucester owes its origin to Birmingham Quaker corn merchants, anxious for rapid transit of their goods to a port. Of the Sturge brothers, we met (page 8), Joseph, one of the early directors of the London & Birmingham, and John who was in 1833 with John Ellis and Captain Moorsom experimenting on smoke in Glenfield tunnel. Two other brothers were Charles (1801-1888) and Edmund (1808-1893).

In or soon after 1830 the Sturge brothers engaged Brunel to survey a route which would get their corn to Gloucester quickly without the distraction of intermediate stopping places. The cost proved too high and the matter dropped. The Birmingham & Gloucester was incorporated in 1836: the proposed route still avoided towns and an outraged Cheltenham resulted in a revision which could approach the town 'as nearly as should be consistent with the interests' of the company. But it still avoided Worcester. By the time the line opened in 1840 the 18-member board was in disarray on a number of issues, notably that of Sunday trains, over which the chairman resigned – though also because of his continued disagreements with Charles Sturge.

In 1841 Captain C. R. Moorsom joined the board, immediately becoming chairman and reducing it in size to a few executive directors, Charles Sturge being responsible for locomotives and Joseph Gibbins (1787-1870), another Birmingham Quaker, for finance.

Meanwhile, the Great Western, with Brunel's 7-foot gauge, was opened from London as far as Maidenhead in 1838 and right through to Bristol in 1841. That year the broad gauge Cheltenham & Great Western Union began running from Swindon to Kemble and Cirencester, though it was 1845 before the rest of the line from Kemble to Gloucester was ready. Another company, the Bristol & Gloucester, had been planned as a standard gauge line, but, seeing the prospect of broad gauge at both their termini, they changed to broad before the line opened in 1844.

At the Birmingham end, the Birmingham & Gloucester shared a terminus with the London & Birmingham and the Grand Junction, which connected with the Liverpool & Manchester and the North Union, leading in turn to the Lancaster & Preston. And in 1842 there was a direct link at Birmingham with the Birmingham & Derby Junction with all its links in the north-east. Caught between a growing standard gauge system to the north and a powerful broad gauge management to the south, the Birmingham & Gloucester was in an unenviable position.

The transhipment due to the change of gauge at Gloucester was causing chaos as this 1844 engraving so vividly depicts.

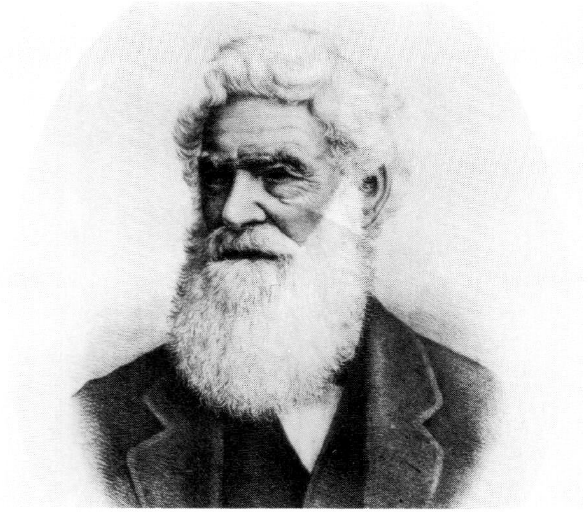

Meanwhile, in 1843, Moorsom had resigned the chairmanship. His place was taken by Samuel Bowly (1802-1884), a Quaker from Cirencester who had settled as a cheese factor in Gloucester in the late 1820s. Though a moderate and genial man (as his portrait here shows) he was also an assiduous collector of hard facts, whether on slavery or temperance, joint stock banks or railways. He quickly paid tribute to Moorsom and also those directors loyal to Moorsom's system but who were now willing to work with and accept the new.

The Bristol & Gloucester had soon realised that its agreement with the Great Western had been a disaster and that amalgamation with the Birmingham & Gloucester was its only hope: a formal agreement between the two was signed on 14 January 1845. The two companies now felt strong enough to negotiate with the Great Western but the company's offer to a deputation on 24 January was felt to be insufficient and a further meeting was arranged.

It has often been told how two directors of the Birmingham & Gloucester were travelling to London by the London & Birmingham on 29 January when, at Rugby, John Ellis entered the carriage (or, in some accounts, a stranger later identified as John Ellis). The three discovered a mutual interest in railways: the Birmingham & Gloucester directors spoke of their mission and Ellis, as deputy chairman of the newly-formed Midland, told them to come to him if they were dissatisfied with the Great Western's terms.

But the two directors were the Birmingham Quakers Edmund Sturge and Joseph Gibbins (one of the latter's nephews later married one of Samuel Bowly's nieces) and Ellis, as we have seen, was a Leicester Quaker. They knew one another well and on 29 January 1845 all three should have been attending Warwick Leicester & Rutland Quarterly Meeting at Coventry. They could have done so and still travelled on the 4.47 pm from Coventry due Euston at 9.0 pm. John Ellis's journal (still extant in 1914) might settle the matter. He cannot have been unaware of the situation nor can he have contemplated a change of gauge at Birmingham with equanimity.

Certain it is that the Midland won the day and stretched its tentacles to Bristol.

The timetable is from *Bradshaw's railway companion*, 1843.

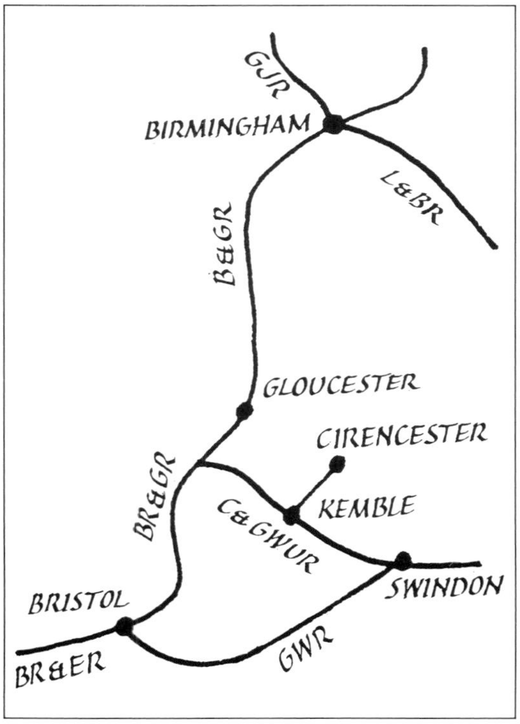

15 **BIRMINGHAM AND GLOUCESTER—53 Miles in length.**

Miles	DOWN TRAINS.	BIRMINGHAM TO GLOUCESTER. 1 mail	2 mail	3	4	5	6	GOODS.		Fares. 1 Cls.	2 Cls	3 Cls
		a.m	a.m	a.m	p.m	p.m	p.m.	a.m.	p.m.	s. d.	s. d.	s. d.
	Depart from BIRMINGHAM..	12 44	3 10	8 45	12 15	2 45	7 15	5 15	3 45			
6	Lifford, arrival at..	..	..	9 2	..	..	7 33	5 53	4 23	1 6	1 0	0 6
12	Blackwell, do	..	..	9 19	..	..	7 51	6 19	4 49	3 0	2 0	1 0
15	Bromsgrove, do ..	1 29	3 55	9 31	12 58	3 31	8 4	6 35	5 5	3 6	2 6	1 6
17	Stoke Works, do..	..	..	9 38	..	..	8 14	6 42	5 12	4 6	3 0	2 0
20	Droitwich, do	1 43	4 9	9 45	1 12	3 46	8 21	6 50	5 20	5 6	4 0	2 0
26	Spetchley, do	2 1	4 27	10 0	1 26	4 0	8 38	7 25	6 0	—	—	—
‡	Wor'ster, by coach	2 31	4 57	10 30	2 0	4 34	9 12	8 10	7 0	7 0	4 6	2 6
33	Defford, arrival at	..	..	10 20	1 48	4 20	8 58	8 10	6 42	8 6	5 6	3 6
34	Eckington, do	..	..	10 25	..	..	9 4	8 15	6 47	9 0	6 0	3 6
37	Bredon do........	..	..	10 33	..	4 29	9 14	8 30	6 57	9 6	6 6	4 0
39	Ashchurch, do	2 38	5 4	10 40	2 5	4 38	9 22	8 50	7 5	10 0	7 0	4 6
	Tewksbury, branch	2 53	5 19	11 55	2 23	4 56	9 50	9 8	..	10 6	7 6	4 0
46	CHELTENHAM	2 56	5 22	11 7	2 26	5 0	9 44	9 20	8 5	12 0	9 0	5 0
53	GLOUCESTER..	3 14	5 40	11 30	2 45	5 20	10 10	9 55	8 30	14 0	10 6	5 6

Miles	UP TRAINS.	GLOUCESTER TO BIRMINGHAM. 1	2	3	4	5 mail	6 mail	GOODS.		Fares. 1 Cls.	2 Cls	3 Cls
		a.m.	a.m.	p.m	p.m	p.m	p.m.	a.m.	p.m.	s. d.	s. d.	s. d.
	Depart from GLOUCESTER..	8 15	11 15	1 0	4 0	7 15	9 0	5 15	4 15			
7	Cheltenham, arrival	8 31	11 31	1 16	4 16	7 35	9 20	5 40	4 50	2 0	1 6	0 8
14	Ashchurch, do	8 50	11 50	1 35	4 35	7 51	9 36	6 1	5 13	3 0	2 6	1 6
	Tewksbury, branch	9 8	12 8	1 52	4 56	8 6	9 50	6 16	..	3 0	2 6	1 6
16	Bredon, arrival at	8 57	..	..	4 43	..	..	6 9	5 21	4 0	3 0	1 6
19	Eckington, do	9 5	..	1 48	4 51	..	..	6 17	5 31	5 0	3 6	2 0
20	Defford, do	9 10	12 3	1 53	4 56	..	..	6 22	5 36	5 0	3 6	2 0
27	Spetchley, do	9 31	12 29	2 12	5 16	8 31	10 16	7 5	6 30	—	—	—
‡	Wor'ster, by coach	10 5	1 3	2 46	5 50	9 1	10 46	8 10	7 0	7 6	5 0	3 6
33	Droitwich, arrival	9 50	12 48	2 31	5 35	8 48	10 33	7 38	7 5	9 0	6 0	3 6
36	Stoke Works, do..	9 59	..	2 39	5 42	..	..	7 48	7 15	9 0	6 0	3 6
38	Bromsgrove, do ..	10 6	1 5	2 46	5 56	9 4	10 49	7 59	7 25	9 6	6 6	4 0
41	Blackwell, do	10 25	..	..	6 6	..	..	8 15	7 40	10 6	7 0	4 6
47	Lifford, do........	10 42	..	..	6 22	..	..	8 40	8 10	12 0	8 0	5 0
53	BIRMINGHAM..	11 7	1 56	3 36	6 45	9 45	11 30	9 35	9 10	14 0	10 6	5 6

Passengers booked between London and Worcester, Cheltenham, and Gloucester, via London and Birmingham Line.

FROM LONDON.

By the train which leaves Euston station at 6 a.m. (1st and 2nd class), proceeding from Birmingham at a quarter past 12.

By the trains leaving Euston station at 8 (mixed,) ¼ to 9, & ¼ to 10 a.m. (mail & 1st class), proceeding from Birmingham at a ¼ before 3. At 11 a.m. and 1¼ p.m., proceeding from Birmingham at 7¼ p.m.; also by the mail train at 8½ p.m., proceeding from Birmingham 3 10 a.m.

TO LONDON.

By the train which leaves Gloucester at a quarter past 8 in the morning, arriving in London at 6 p.m. (1st & 2nd class.)

By the train which leaves Gloucester at 1 p.m. arriving in London at 9¼ p.m. (1st class) or by the 6 p.m. from Birmingham, arriving in London at 11¼ p.m. By the Mail train leaving Gloucester at 9 at night, arriving in London at ½ past 5 a.m. (1st and 2nd class.)

The London Company's trains leave Birmingham for London at 10 a.m., 12 noon, 2 15, 4 p.m., and 12 night.

The Grand Junction Company's trains leave Birmingham for Liverpool and Manchester at 1¾ & 11½ a.m., 2¼, (4½ to Liverpool only,) and 7¼ p.m.

The Derby Company's trains leave Birmingham for Derby at 12 30, 7, & 10½ a.m. 1 25, 4, and 6 25 p.m.

Coaches leave Worcester for Malvern, Ledbury, & Hereford, at 11 a.m. & 4 45 p.m.

ONLY THE MAIL TRAINS RUN ON SUNDAYS.

* From Cheltenham to Gloucester, 10¼ a.m. and 6¼ p.m.; from Gloucester to Cheltenham, 9¾ and 5¾ p.m.

Coaches leave Gloucester for Bristol at 3½, and 6 morning; at 12, 2¾, 3¼, and 5¼ afternoon; Bath direct 2¾ p.m.; for Taunton, Exeter, &c., at 3½ and 6 morning; for Chepstow, Newport, Cardiff, and Swansea, every Tuesday, Thursday, and Saturday mornings at 9; for Ross, Monmouth, Ragland, Abergavenny, Brecon, Merthy, Llandilo, Llandovery, and Caermarthen, every morning at 4½.

SOME EARLY QUAKER PASSENGERS

R. Barclay Fox (1817-1855) of Falmouth, after travelling to Exeter by coach, journeys by overnight train to Paddington, 9-10 February 1843:

> The night-air was very sharp & my railway companions were emphatically dull, which was however a relief after incessant chattering all the day. Emerged from the great movement at 5 in the morning, charmed to a due pitch of patriotism with the advantages of steam conveyance. A railway train is a dusky piece of utilitarianism to look at & yet it is not without poetry, particularly when in motion...

> Look at the magician in front, a grimy potentate in fustian & corduroys called by men the Engineer. He has harnessed to his car a mighty & unseen Strength & drives him on with his ponderous load behind him at the rate of 30 miles an hour. You hear his giant breath as he rushes through the murk. You have no thought of fear, although given up, life & limb, to this terrific guidance, & more helpless than an infant; & dream not of thanking Heaven for your preservation when you return to men after a weird ride of 200 miles through the darkness.

William Lucas (1804-1851) of Hitchin travels on 19 April 1849:

> After dinner in one horse Fly to Bedford and by train at five minutes to six to Bletchley where I met W. Clay and proceeded with him to Rugby; after waiting here about an hour, by favour, we were allowed to proceed to Derby in one of the holiday trains now so much in fashion. It conveyed a most noisy company and the scenes of uproarious merriment at the refreshment rooms made us glad to part company at Derby, where we slept.

The Bedford Railway, connecting that town with Bletchley, had been opened in 1846. The same year it was amalgamated with the London & Birmingham and others to form the London & North Western. The proposed Leicester & Bedford, of which William Lucas was a director, came to nothing, negotiations with George Hudson having failed. The Midland's extension from Leicester to Bedford and Hitchin was not opened until 1857.

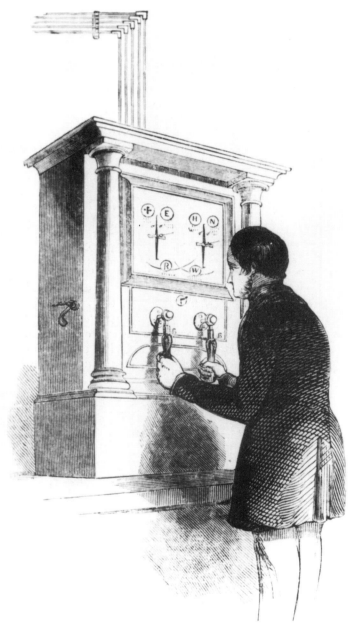

John Tawell (1784-1845) of Beccles, Suffolk, came to London to work in a drapery business and, aged 23, became a Quaker. But, alas, within 14 months he was disowned for 'disorderly and unchaste conduct'. He was married about this time, continued to wear Quaker garb, and was known as a Quaker in his new employment as traveller for a Cheapside firm of wholesale druggists.

At the age of 30 he was convicted for forgery and sentenced to transportation. Arrived at Sydney in 1815, he worked hard, obtained an emancipation ticket, and set up in business as a chemist and grocer. The business prospered and in 1831 the family returned to England. He made a couple of business trips back to Australia in the next few years and in 1835 built at his own expense a meeting house for Sydney Friends.

In 1838 his wife died. During her illness she had been nursed by Sarah Hart, who became Tawell's mistress: he later supported her in a cottage at Salt Hill, near Slough. After his second marriage, in 1841, problems arose and on New Year's Day 1845 he travelled to Slough, administered poison to Sarah and, as he thought, made a safe getaway by the London train.

He was apparently unaware of the invention of the electric telegraph and, as the news-cutting shows, this ignorance was his undoing. An unfortunate passenger, John Tawell deserves remembrance here as the first person to be arrested as a result of this new technology. He was hanged at Aylesbury on 25 March 1845.

...We went to see the Electric Telegraph at Slough, one of the most wonderful adaptations of science which this inventive age brought forth. By means of this a conversation, if the apparatus is put up, can be carried on by persons at opposite ends of the Island, without difficulty or loss of time. It will no doubt be productive of important results.

William Lucas, 10 July 1845

for town last night by the 7.42 train. I despatched orders by the telegraph to have the prisoner watched on his arrival at Paddington. A few minutes afterwards an answer was returned, stating that the suspected party had arrived, and that Sergeant Williams had left the terminus in the same omnibus for the City.

The words of the communication were precisely as follows :—

THE MESSAGE.

A murder has just been committed at Salt Hill, and the suspected murderer was seen to take a first-class ticket for London by the train which left Slough at 7h. 42m. p.m. He is in the garb of a Quaker, with a brown great coat on, which reaches nearly down to his feet; he is in the last compartment of the second first-class carriage.

THE REPLY.

The up-train has arrived; and a person answering, in every respect, the description given by telegraph came out of the compartment mentioned. I pointed the man out to Sergeant Williams. The man got **into** *a New-road omnibus, and Sergeant Williams into the same.*

The maps above and to the right are from the annual Quaker *Book of meetings* for 1845 and 1855: the 10-year comparison is instructive but, alas, the maps are not as accurate as could be wished.

Passenger: 'One who travels or is carried in some vessel or vehicle, esp. on board ship, … by coach, and by railway, tramway or the like' (*Oxford English Dictionary*). Let us hope that British Rail will overcome its obsession with that word 'customer' and recognise that it is responsible for conveying goods (things) and passengers (people).

GEORGE BRADSHAW & HIS TIMETABLE

George Bradshaw (1801–1853) was born at Windsor Bridge, Salford, and on leaving school was apprenticed to a Manchester engraver. In 1820 (about the time that he joined Friends) the family moved to Belfast where George set up in business. Within two years he was back in Manchester where he specialised in the engraving of maps. From 1829 he produced a series of regional maps of canals which, with permission, he dedicated to Telford.

It was in 1835 that he added a letterpress printing department to his business and the first known edition (though with a different title) of *Bradshaw's railway companion* is dated 1839. Herbert Spencer and others, however, have given persuasive grounds for recollecting an issue the previous year. The *Companion* was designed, in the words of R. D. Kay, editor of it and the *Guide* from the outset to 1880, in 'a form and size suitable for the waistcoat pocket'.

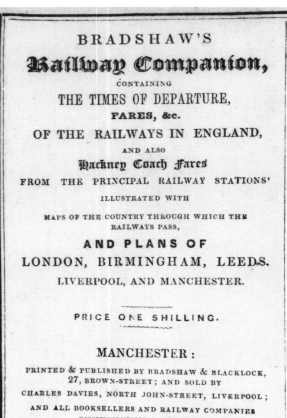

Apart from the departure sheet reproduced on page 7, the Liverpool & Manchester had as early as 1831 published a 12-page booklet, planned by James Cropper who claimed it as the origin of Bradshaw. Less than a page of it was sufficient for train times, eight pages being filled with details of connecting coaches and two with information on steam packets. The idea of a timetable with intermediate stations and arrivals was discussed by Bradshaw and other Friends as they walked home from Manchester Meeting.

In 1841 there appeared in larger format *Bradshaw's railway guide* which, published monthly though without the engraved maps of the *Companion,* was to oust it in popularity, the last issue of the *Companion* being in 1848. The 'shareholders' guide' (later *Bradshaw's railway manual*) was first published for that year, continuing until the issue for 1923: it is an invaluable means of tracking railway directors (someone ought to compile a *Biographical dictionary of railway directors 1821-60,* even if the task up to 1847 would be laborious).

If Bradshaw was successful in delegating day-to-day work to his staff he kept his finger firmly on the railway pulse and could write on 26 June 1850 to his London agent: 'The South Wales Railway is now open from Chepstow to Swansea, and we have not been furnished with a time bill. Please send to their office, 446 Strand, for one and let us have it by return'.

Edgar B. Collinson (1868-1956), whose portrait is shown above, was a master at Ackworth 1899-1930. Four of his pupils recall his Bradshaw tests:

J. Stanley Carr: 'Then there was Accounts period on Saturday morning. On the blackboard was the exercise in "Bradshaw" for next week:- "Strome Ferry dep. 12.2 pm to Stratford-on-Avon". He always chose tricky ones, generally alliterative. We corrected last week's effort: Windermere dep. 9.20 am, and so on to the journey's end, with special marks for restaurant car, sleeper, and change of stations'.

Donald Birkett: 'EBC was also known for his lessons in Bradshaw; and what a weighty tome it was, before the days of Lord Beeching. The boy who came out top was the one who could find boats and trains from the Outer Hebrides to remote places on the South Coast or West Country in the quickest time and at the lowest cost, meals included, but no overnight hotels if sleepers could be found'.

Stanley Horner: 'I had no liking for Bradshaw'.

Eric Bellingham: 'And those Bradshaws: Forty-four of them; one in each boy's desk. What better discipline for boys, most of whom would later be enteing commercial or professional offices, than to master Bradshaw and thus add to the pleasure and confidence with which to make a cross-country railway journey. Not for Ackworth boys the colourless bare bones of an ABC or the prejudiced orientation of a local railway guide'.

Duncan Fairn (1906-1986), a prison commissioner and Quaker, once described 'the educated man or woman' as 'one who can follow the Anglican service from the prayer book with intelligence, plot a cross-country journey from Bradshaw and get there, and can undress on the beach with discretion'. When he repeated these words in his 1951 Swarthmore Lecture the Anglican *Alternative service book* was nearly 30 years in the future. By that time discretion on the beach was barely a relevant issue. And Duncan Fairn was not to know that after a mere decade Bradshaw, with its issue 1521 in June 1961, would pass from the scene.

Bradshaw's main concern was for international peace. The American philanthropist and peace advocate Elihu Burritt has described how on a train journey from Manchester to Bolton, 23 February 1848, the suggestion was made of an international peace congress at Paris that summer, and how Bradshaw immediately reached for a pencil and accurately calculated travel costs on the crown of his hat. In the event, that revolutionary year was not a propitious one and the congress was held there in 1849, Bradshaw making travel arrangements for special trains and steamer for 700 delegates. That conference, presided over by Victor Hugo, was followed by Frankfurt (1850) and others.

In 1849 Bradshaw reprinted Thomas Clarkson's *Life of William Penn,* with an essay by W. E. Forster (he of the 1870 Education Act) refuting the criticisms of Macaulay. The book announced Bradshaw's intension of bringing out a series of cheap editions of standard Friends' literature should sufficient encouragement be given, but this does not seem to have been followed further.

In 1853 he went to Christiania (Oslo) to visit an old Manchester acquaintance, now manager of the Norwegian railway, but while there he contracted cholera and on 6 September died at the age of 53.

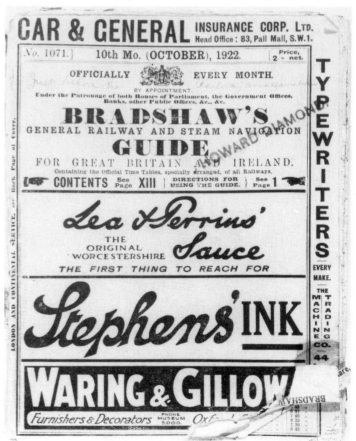

THOMAS EDMONDSON & THE RAILWAY TICKET

Thomas Edmondson (1792-1851), whose portrait is shown here, was born in Lancaster, son of a Quaker trunk-maker. His younger brother George, who in 1819 joined his fellow-Quaker Daniel Wheeler in draining the marshes near Petersburg at the invitation of the Czar of Russia, was later master of Tulketh Academy, near Blackburn, and of Queenwood College, Hampshire. Thomas's elder brother Joseph (1788-1861) was master at the meeting house schools at Penketh and, later, Bolton-le-Moors: in 1821 John Bright had been his pupil but had not warmed to him, and another pupil, Joseph Crosfield of Liverpool, described him as 'not a good school master; an irritable, illtempered man with an imperfect digestion'. We shall return to him shortly.

Thomas, after an apprenticeship at Gillows & Co., Lancaster, became a cabinet maker and upholsterer at Carlisle, but the business went into bankruptcy. In 1837 he was appointed station master at Milton (later Brampton Junction) on the Newcastle & Carlisle. He was uneasy at discovering that passengers paid him their fare without obtaining a satisfactory receipt. He was even more uneasy at discovering that he was, in accord with stage coach practice, to hand the money over to the guard without obtaining a satisfactory receipt. He therefore started writing previously-numbered tickets and the following year moved from paper to card and used a simple form of printing.

The Newcastle & Carlisle directors did not seem to him interested in following up this idea and in 1839 he accepted an invitation to join the Manchester & Leeds (precursor of the Lancashire & Yorkshire) at double the salary.

In December 1839 a deputation from the Birmingham & Gloucester (it was the Quakers Sturge and Gibbins once again) visited the Manchester & Leeds and were especially interested in its rolling stock and its system of fares for passengers, reporting that the 'System of Ticketing for Passengers is both more economical and a greater security against frauds on the Company than any other we have seen'. The Birmingham & Gloucester adopted the Edmondson system (card for the tickets was supplied half by Bradshaw and half by the firm of De la Rue). Thomas's brother Joseph, together with Joseph's son John then aged about 16, entered the service of the Birmingham & Gloucester for a few years.

Meanwhile, in 1841, Thomas set up business as a ticket printer, Joseph joining him in 1844. By then 30 of

the 40 companies operating in Britain were using Edmondson tickets, the Stockton & Darlington adopting them that year. By 1847, 74 of the 80 companies were using them and Joseph's sons John and Thomas set up a branch office in Dublin. Thomas's son, John Beeby Edmondson (1831-1887) also joined the firm, continuing in it till his death. The firm itself lasted until 1960.

The *Illustrated London news* of 22 February 1845 devoted a full page to the Edmondson ticket, its illustration of the printing machine being reproduced here: 'The whole of this very beautiful apparatus is worked by a hand-lever, printing at every stroke a ticket bearing a consecutive number, and discharging it in a receiver below'.

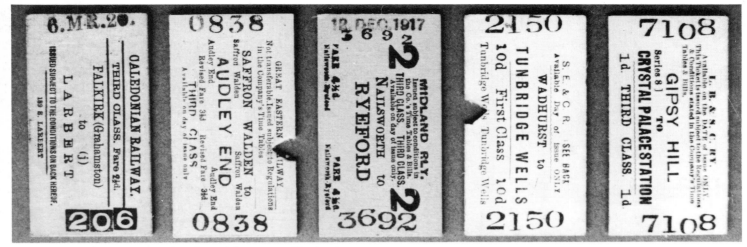

During the 1860s Friends with evangelical views were in the ascendant among British Quakers, but in Manchester meeting there was a vigorous and vocal group of liberals sympathetic to the Anglican symposium *Essays and reviews* (1860) popularly known as 'the seven against Christ'. J. B. Edmondson, who was assistant clerk to Hardshaw East Monthly Meeting and an overseer, expressed in the late 1860s his disbelief in some of the biblical miracles, causing vast alarm among the ministers and elders of the meeting and provoking repressive reaction.

Bradshaw's son William married one of J. B. Edmondson's daughters: there was an only child, Hilda, who died unmarried in 1959. There are plenty of descendants of Bradshaw and a sufficiency of those of Edmondson – but it would have been pleasant had there been those who could claim both men as ancestors.

These tickets are from the collection of Redford Crosfield Harris (1902-1980), a London chartered accountant, sometime treasurer of the British & Foreign Bible Society and chairman of the governers of Leighton Park School, clerk of the Yearly Meeting of British Quakers 1949-53. He was great-grandson of the Joseph Crosfield who took such a dislike to Joseph Edmondson's schoolmastering. Railways have, throughout their history, always claimed enthusiasts, whether on locomotive design or station architecture or the logging of journeys, whether photographers or collectors of tickets. Let Redford stand for all those enthusiasts.

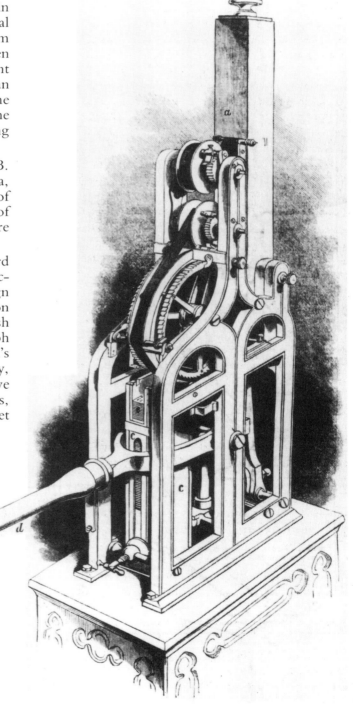

RANSOMES & MAY

In 1789 Robert Ransome (1753-1830), a Quaker ironmaster from Norwich, started a foundry in a disused maltings in the middle of Ipswich with a capital of £200 and a single workman. The patenting in 1803 of his chilled ploughshare and in 1808 of a method of interchangeable plough parts laid the foundations of a business important in British agricultural history.

Business was booming and in 1809 Ransome's son James (1782-1849) joined the firm, followed three years later by the civil engineer William Cubitt (1785-1861), whom we must be careful not to claim among the Quakers. The firm now expanded to include bridge-building and later the provision of Ipswich's gas supply. This diversification was the firm's salvation in the agricultural slump which followed the Napoleonic wars. Cubitt left in 1826 but retained informal links with the firm, which included some early railway work: Kings Cross station, incidentally, is by Lewis Cubitt, William's nephew.

Cubitt's departure left a gap which was ably filled by the arrival in 1836 of Charles May (1801-1860) who came from remarkable families on both sides. His father was a draper but earlier generations had been Quaker clock-makers in Henley-on-Thames and Witney (which may help explain his engineering acumen). His mother was of the Curtis family of Alton, well-known as apothecaries and botanists (William of *Curtis's botanical magazine* was her first cousin). Charles's younger brother Francis will be best known for Bryant & May matches.

Charles May was responsible for work arising from the railway boom, concentrating on chairs and fastenings in rail laying, for which a patent was taken out in 1841. From 1846 to 1852 the firm was styled Ransomes & May and the balance sheet for 1851 valued agricultural work at £35,000 and railway and other work at £87,000. May left the firm shortly after this and in 1869 all railway work was transfered to the new firm of Ransomes & Rapier.

The engineer of 16 January 1857 shows Ransomes' method of tipping the treenails which secured both the rails to the chairs and the chairs to the sleepers: one man and a boy could produce 1,200 an hour. During 1866 over a million left the works.

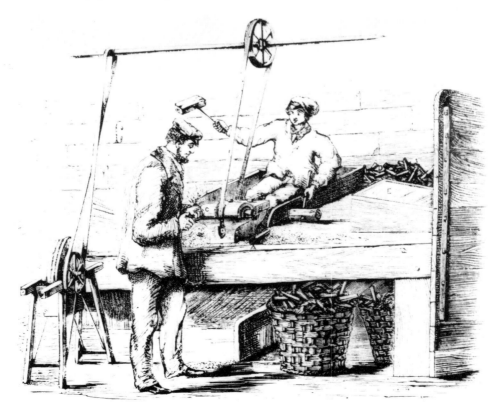

1854 CLARKS &
THE SOMERSET CENTRAL

In the west country the Bristol & Exeter reached Bridgwater in 1841, Taunton next year and Yeovil in 1853, while the Great Western got to Frome in 1850. But mid-Somerset was still railwayless.

The Quaker brothers Cyrus Clark (1801-1866) and James (1811-1906) had entered into partnership in 1833. The fellmongering and sheepskin rug business at Street, three miles from Glastonbury, extended to wool-lined slippers and then shoes: it was rapidly expanding and was hampered for want of a railway. A public meeting in Glastonbury town hall on 16 September 1850 led to the official opening of the Somerset Central from that town to Highbridge on 28 August 1854, extending to Burnham (for South Wales) in 1858.

In 1859 Glastonbury to Wells was opened and in 1862 a line southeastwards to link with the Dorset Central, which had opened in 1860. In 1862 came amalgamation as the Somerset & Dorset and the following year the completed track enabled through running coast to coast from Poole to Burnham. In 1874 the line from Evercreech to Bath was opened, thus linking with the Midland which, jointly with the London & South Western, leased the line in 1889.

James and Cyrus Clark and Columbus Clothier were founder directors, James Clark continuing until 1889. 'This proved', he recollected, 'an engagement involving far more responsibility than I ever contemplated, and I was very thankful at last to be relieved from responsibility

when the working was made over to two strong companies who could develop the traffick'. James Clark (whose portrait is shown here) was first cousin to Joseph Sturge (see page 7) and they were together at the international peace congresses at Brussels in 1848 and Frankfurt in 1850.

C. & J. Clark Ltd organised centenary celebrations for 28 August 1954 when more than 100 of the 250 living descendants of James Clark were among the 600-700 passengers on a special train whose arrival at Burnham is pictured here: it was remarked that 'few railway centenaries have been celebrated with such gusto'. The line, however, had after the 1948 nationalisation become a pawn in inter-regional adjustments: it was being steadily run down and closure was announced for 7 March 1966.

LONDON & NORTH WESTERN

The London & North Western had been formed in 1846, drawing together the London & Birmingham, the Manchester & Birmingham and the Grand Junction, which had the previous year absorbed the Liverpool & Manchester. It was in connection with the Liverpool & Manchester that we met, on page 7, Thomas Clarke Worsdell: we must now turn to his three sons, Nathaniel, Thomas and George.

George Worsdell (1821-1912) was educated at Tulketh Hall, near Blackburn, the school run by Thomas Edmondson's brother George. He developed railway and engineering skills in London, Swindon and Hull, and in 1845 set up for himself in Warrington where at the Dallam Forge he produced the first rolled bar iron in Lancashire. At the 1851 Great Exhibition he won a gold medal 'for excellence of iron and of railway plant'. A partnership at the works was not successful and was perhaps the main cause of his bankruptcy in 1858. At this time the insomnia began which was to dog him for the rest of his life and which was also to afflict his son Edward, a teacher and a significant figure in the Quaker renaissance of the later 19th century and whose *The gospel of divine help* (1886) was to become a minor theological classic.

Thomas Worsdell (1818-1893) had in his teens won a prize of £200 offered for the best model of a carriage to be adopted by the London & Birmingham. It was in this model that his screw coupling was first employed. By 1845 he had settled in Birmingham, starting an engineering works in which were trained the Quaker Tangye brothers, later famous for their Cornwall Works. He was preoccupied with rail safety, his first patent being an apparatus 'for protecting the passengers from injury in the case of collision'; he also devised a means of letting down the sides of goods waggons to allow horses and cattle to be detrained by means of a ramp. On his retirement in 1867 he and his wife became members of Swarthmoor meeting, near Ulverston, Lancashire.

It is the eldest, Nathaniel (1809-1886), who concerns us most. After working with his father on the Liverpool & Manchester he succeeded him as superintendent of the carriage department in 1836, when T. C. Worsdell left for Germany to become carriage builder for the Leipzig & Dresden. In 1837 Nathaniel invented an apparatus (first tried out at Winsford, just north of Crewe) for picking up and depositing mail bags: it was patented the following year.

Nathaniel Worsdell (whose portrait is above) made no money from the invention. The Post Office showed great interest in buying out his patent but turned down his £3,500 asking price (considered too low by a Patent Office official), offering £500 and rejecting his reduced price of £1,500. It then introduced its own form of pick up and set down apparatus for mail bags – a moral infringement of patent though, lacking some of Worsdell's refinements, unsatisfactory until modifications akin to Worsdell's were made when his patent expired in 1852. It is not a nice story. A reconstruction of one of Worsdell's 1838 travelling post offices (in the National Railway Museum, York) is pictured below.

In 1838 (the year the Manchester & Leeds appointed him consultative inspector of carriages) he built the *Enterprise* coach for the Liverpool & Manchester, comprising three horse-carriage bodies on a railway truck, thus establishing the compartment coach so long to be near universal in Britain. In 1843 he became manager of the Grand Junction's coach-making department, continuing at Crewe with the London & North Western until retirement in 1881, having been responsible from 1865 for the stock purchasing department. He was a member of Nantwich meeting until retirement took him to Birkenhead: he was recorded a minister in 1865.

Of the nine children surviving childhood, three sons belong to our story. All were at Ackworth and one,

Thomas William (1838-1916), went on to George Edmondson's, by then at Queenwood College, Hampshire. He then alternated between Crewe (timber yard and locomotive department) and his uncle Thomas's engineering works at Birmingham until 1865 when he emigrated to the United States, working with the Pennsylvania Railroad until 1871. He then returned to Crewe as works manager until 1881 when he joined the Great Eastern, where we shall meet him again.

Edwin (1845-1930) worked for a timber importer in Liverpool until in 1866 he married a professional dancer – to the family's dismay and Hardshaw West Monthly Meeting's disapprobation. He emigrated, becoming a backwoodsman farmer in Iowa until, incapacitated by sunstroke, he returned to England and the London & North Western's permanent way department, being manager of the Garston works on retirement in 1910. He then settled in Kendal, taking an active part in the meeting's life until his death.

Wilson (1850-1920) was in the drawing office at Crewe for six months before joining the Pennsylvania Railroad in 1867. He returned to England about 1871 and was with the London & North Western until 1883 (locomotive erecting shop and drawing office at Crewe, assistant foreman at Stafford sheds, foreman at Wolverhampton and in charge at Chester sheds). In 1883 he joined the North Eastern, where we shall meet him again.

LATER DAYS ON THE MIDLAND

We saw (page 9) that by the time John Ellis relinquished the chairmanship of the Midland in 1858 it had secured a route to London by its extension to Hitchin and thus over Great Northern metals to Kings Cross. By the time of his death in 1862 it was painfully clear that the Great Northern was putting as many obstacles as possible in the way of Midland trains. An independent route to London was becoming essential. It was achieved during the chairmanship of another Leicester Quaker, William Evans Hutchinson (1806-1882).

In 1839 Hutchinson, a chemist and druggist, had been appointed superintendent and manager of the Midland Counties. He made all arrangements for its opening and working and it was remarked that it 'was especially gratifying to find that although [he] was without practical experience, the arrangements of this quiet, meditative little gentleman were most successful'. He resigned his appointment in 1840 and was then appointed a director (he was already on the board of the Leicester & Swannington), continuing with the Midland until his death: he was chairman 1864-70. It was 1868 when St Pancras was opened – the unprecedented 243-foot span of W. H. Barlow's train shed later frouted by George Gilbert Scott's Italian brick Gothic hotel. No wonder that John Betjeman described it as 'a temple to the age of steam'.

John Ellis's son Edward Shipley Ellis (1817-1879) was chairman of the Midland from 1873 until his death. He had been 15 years old when the Leicester & Swannington was opened and had come under George Stephenson's spell. He was emphatic, and reiterated, that 'the Midland system had become so important, and its continued success so essential to the well-being of its shareholders, as well as the commerce of the country, that its affairs, its policy, administration, and management must absorb the whole commercial life of the men at its head, including that of its chairman'.

He tried hard to enforce and ensure 'punctuality in the running of trains and civility and attention on the part of the servants of the company'. Late running he regarded as a discourtesy and he was concerned that there should be enough spare engines and crews to deal with emergencies. It proved to be good public relations and therefore good business as well.

Though 3rd class passengers no longer had to travel in the open waggons of early days they were still discriminated against. They were debarred by most

companies from as many as half – and in some cases two-thirds – of scheduled trains, yet in 1870 3rd class represented 75% of railway travel. In 1872, the year before Edward Ellis became chairman, the Midland board permitted 3rd class passengers to use all trains, the Great Eastern acting similarly: it was not until 1890 that the Great Western followed suit.

In 1854 the Great North of Scotland opened with only 1st and 3rd but when in 1872 the Midland board proposed the abolition of 2nd class and the upgrading of 3rd, Ellis had to face an angry meeting of shareholders, as was recalled 25 years later:

> No one who was present at the meeting of Midland shareholders in November 1874 will ever forget the fierce way in which the proposal to abolish second-class was assailed: nor the able way in which Mr Ellis quietly marshalled the facts and announced the determination of the directors to stand by their policy, notwithstanding the great pressure which

had been brought to bear by other companies. It was the most notable and memorable railway meeting during the last quarter of a century. A weaker man would have yielded before the storm. Mr Ellis, by his firmness and strength of purpose, as well as the grasp which he had of all the facts and his confidence in the soundness of his judgment, carried the day; and twenty-six years' experience has verified the soundness of his position.

He had been elected to the Leicester town council at the age of 25 and was mayor in 1860. He was active in the management of the Wyggeston Schools and Wyggeston Hospital Charity; and when he was chairman of the new waterworks it was largely due to his foresight and unremitting energy that, in one particularly dry season, Leicester escaped an imminent water famine with its attendant toll of disease and infant mortality.

In the first 35 years of the Midland there was a Quaker chairman for 21, and it was said that the 'board was accustomed to arrive at its decisions by "the opinion of the meeting" after the Quaker manner rather than by a simple majority'.

This sketch, by Henry Newman (1818-1908) of Leominster, is of the 1768 meeting house in Soar Lane, Leicester, which continued in use until 1876. It is the meeting house where John Ellis worshipped and, for most of their lives, William E. Hutchinson and Edward S. Ellis.

27

GREAT EASTERN

The Eastern Counties opened to Romford in 1839 and Colchester in 1843. Between that year and 1845 Nathaniel Worsdell's brother Thomas appears to have worked briefly at the Stratford works of the Northern & Eastern, which ran from Stratford to Broxbourne in 1840 and Hertford in 1843. Taken over by the Eastern Counties it opened through Cambridge to Norwich in 1845, connecting with a line to Yarmouth. Joseph John Gurney, Norwich banker and brother to Elizabeth Fry, was in Cumberland when he received a home letter from his son dated 30 July 1845: 'The Railroad opened yesterday – I believe auspiciously – My uncle [Henry] Birkbeck went up by it & I believe my Aunt intends to follow tomorrow with Lucy'. A contemporary print depicts Norwich station.

In 1862 the Eastern Counties, having leased or taken over other East Anglian companies, was renamed the Great Eastern. The opening of its new terminus, Liverpool Street, in 1874-5, replacing Bishopsgate, meant the rehousing of some 7,000 people. Parliament required the company to offer 2d fares for the suburban journeys that had now to be considerably stepped up so that 20,000 passengers poured daily into Liverpool Street.

Despite the Stratford works the Great Eastern relied largely on outside contractors for locomotives. During the 1870s an increasing number were built at an improved Stratford works and when in 1881 T. W. Worsdell (1838-1916), son to Nathaniel, became locomotive superintendent he determined that all Great Eastern locomotives should be built there. He began to put system into the works. Among his designs were the Y14 (later LNER J15) 0-6-0s, one of which, no. 699 (1885), is shown here.

In 1885 Worsdell transferred to the North Eastern. He was succeeded by James Holden (1837-1925) who came after 20 years with the Great Western, following earlier years with the York Newcastle & Berwick and the North Eastern. He settled at Snaresbrook and the following year joined the Society of Friends at Wanstead. After late Quaker committee meetings at Devonshire House, Bishopsgate, he would say whimsically that he would 'take an engine home' – preferring a footplate ride on an engine returning light to Stratford to waiting for the next passenger train.

Despite Worsdell's good work at Stratford, Holden (whose portrait is shown here) found plenty of scope for his technical and organising abilities. He had the registers of locomotives and rolling stock overhauled until he was satisfied that they were dependable and he set about reducing the large number of different types of locomotives. He continued with Worsdell's Y14s and in 1886 came the T18 0-6-0 tanks, followed by the T19 2-4-0 express engines (110 built in all). All his locomotives had side-window cabs. His last and most famous design was the Claud Hamilton 4-4-0 (1900): one is shown here on Brentwood bank, piloted by T19 no. 735, built 1888.

He had to wrestle with increasing traffic problems. In 1855 2.14 million had used the old Bishopsgate; in 1902 65.3 million were passing through Liverpool Street. The 20,000 passengers of the late 1870s had in 1902 become 250,000, 90.7% from 12 miles or less. To the original 10 platforms eight more were added in 1894. Holden's problem was to get enough locomotives and carriages for the 399 suburban and 36 main-line trains arriving daily: if, in increasing seating capacity of surburban stock he did not increase comfort, who shall blame him?

He was perhaps proudest of his Stratford dormitory for country enginemen whose rosters involved an overnight stay in London. It opened in 1890 with 20 beds in separate cubicles, 18 being added in 1891 and 12 more in 1899. There were reading, smoking and dining rooms as well as baths. The corridors were heavily padded to reduce noise. Slippers were provided for everyone on entrance so that sleeping men should not be disturbed. He told the *Railway magazine* in 1900 that during the decade the beds had been occupied 150,000 times 'and despite the fact (or perhaps because of it) that there are no regulations as to what a man may or may not do, there have been only eight entries in the complaint book, and those of an unimportant nature, during the whole period'. The rest room is pictured here.

He retired in 1907. As his more strenuous activities needed to be curtailed, he took his exercise in wood-sawing and knife-cleaning, loving to be involved in household tasks until in 1923 infirmity necessitated a removal to his daughter's home at Bath.

LATER DAYS ON THE NORTH EASTERN

Let us, in returning to the North Eastern, look at some engineers.

William J. Cudworth (1849-1909), after schooldays at Stramongate, Kendal, and at Bootham, joined the North Eastern in 1865 as a pupil of his father, William Cudworth, who had begun with the Stockton & Darlington in 1840 under the Quaker engineer John Harris. W. J. Cudworth's uncle, James, had in 1845 been appointed locomotive superintendent of the South Eastern, two years later planning its new works at Ashford, Kent.

After a spell in London studying architecture, WJC was assistant engineer 1874-91 on the North Eastern's central division, engineer of the division 1891-9 and chief engineer of the enlarged southern division 1899-1909. During his term of office automatic signalling was installed between Alne and Thirsk and a new signal box at York contained the largest number of manual levers in Britain. He was also responsible for the Wear Valley Railway, the Selby-Goole line and the Isle of Axholme Joint, including the swing bridge at Crowle.

In 1885 T. W. Worsdell transferred from the Great Eastern to the North Eastern, serving at Gateshead as chief mechanical engineer. He introduced a new system of locomotive classification and his C class 0-6-0s next year (as shown below) had the spacious windows which were to become a standard feature on the North Eastern. He established a tradition of handsome locomotive design, continued by his younger brother Wilson Worsdell (1850-1920) who succeeded him when, on grounds of health, he retired in 1890.

Wilson Worsdell had been appointed assistant mechanical engineer at Gateshead in 1883 under what was to be the short and explosive tenure of Alexander McDonnell. In the interregnum after McDonnell's departure Henry Tennant, as general manager, took overall responsibility for locomotives until TWW's appointment: to this period belong the 2-4-0 'Tennants', which owe much to the ideas of Wilson Worsdell.

On his brother's retirement he found he had to contend with increasing train loads and, in consequence, the need for more powerful engines. He was the first to introduce (1899) the 4-6-0 for passenger work. One of his P3 0-6-0s (shown opposite) is now at work on the North Yorkshire Moors Railway, that stretch of line from Grosmont to Pickering which continues the tradition of the 1835-6 Whitby & Pickering.

Administration was not going so well. The North Eastern had gained the reputation of a company that 'never adopts a change until some more enterprising railway company has convinced the world of its practicability'. Henry Tennant, having retired as general manager in 1891, became a director until his death in 1910. By then he had been 66 years with the company and its predecessors. It was too long. He was an albatross round the neck of George Gibb, the go-ahead general manager 1891-1906. Tennant was the centre of a dissident group of directors, resentful at the way the radical Gibb hobnobbed with economists and statisticians, and perhaps jealous at the success of his reforms – made the easier by the retirement of many of Tennant's long-serving managerial team.

Matters were not helped by the 1902 crisis. Joseph Whitwell Pease (1828-1903), grandson of Edward, had been a director of the Stockton & Darlington and, after 1863, the North Eastern, becoming deputy chairman in 1888 and chairman in 1895. In summer 1902, however, his financial interests collapsed and, as the company did business with his Darlington bank, it was dragged into the highly publicised legal proceedings – and also lost some £125,000.

But at least one man from the old order belonged to the new. Philip Burtt (1862-1931) came from a Lincolnshire farming family: after schooldays at Ackworth he joined the North Eastern in 1877, moving to the general manager's office in 1882. In 1892 he was selected as Gibb's principal assistant and from then on occupied a series of senior posts in the traffic department.

The main lines of organisational change were drawn up at the end of 1900 and, the dissident directors being overruled, Gibb with Wilson Worsdell, Philip Burtt and two others visited the USA, their 31-day tour covering 4000 miles. The changes begun in the 1890s reached their logical conclusion with Burtt's appointment to the new post of general traffic manager, thus ovecoming the system where the goods and passenger departments were each responsible for working their own traffic.

His brother-in-law Frederick H. Graveson (1870-1954) joined the North Eastern in 1894 and was, like Burtt, a 'Gibb man' in his preoccupation with operating statistics and costing: he was with the company 40 years, being at retirement assistant to the London & North Eastern's divisional general manager at York.

Philip Burtt's farming background would out. In 1904 he visited Denmark and on his return established the Wensleydale Pure Milk Society, with the Northallerton Dairy, as part of a campaign for cleaner milk and the promotion of a co-operative. He was also a considerable ornithologist. In 1911 he moved to a subordinate position in the North Eastern's traffic department and three years later, at the age of 52, retired. It was to be an active retirement as we shall see on the next page.

THE TWENTIETH CENTURY

The Railways Act 1921 amalgamated 123 separate companies into 'the big four' (Great Western, London & North Eastern, London Midland & Scottish and Southern). The Transport Act 1947 brought nationalisation. Quaker railway involvement may well have been less than in the 19th century: it was certainly in a different key. Let us look at three individuals.

We have already seen Philip Burtt (whose portrait is shown above) as a North Eastern man. Following his 1914 retirement he lectured at the London School of Economics and was the author of three substantial books – *The principal factors in freight train operating* (1923), *Control on the railways* (1926) and *Railway electrification and traffic problems* (1929). In the second of these

his preoccupation with traffic supervision through 'a centralised and coordinated system of telephones' suggests that he would have warmed to the development of electronics. As for electrification, there were then in Britain some 530 route miles, mainly surburban, and he noted how tunnels in Switzerland and the price of coal in France, Italy and Holland had led to electric power for main lines. His statistical training enabled him to demonstrate the cheaper and better working of electric trains for main lines and to the question 'How is the necessary capital to be found?' he responded unequivocally that government help must be called on.

In a 1921 lecture, referring to the 'exaggerated nature of the competition in pre-war times under which one railway tried to wrest traffic from another, railways tried to take traffic away from coastal steamers and from canals, tramways from light railways, and so on', he urged the need to recognise 'two aspects of inter-dependence: first, the interdependence of the various forms of transport, standard railways, light railways, roadways, canal system, docks and harbours and steamships; and secondly, the interdependence of the welfare of the community and that of the transport agencies of the country taken as a whole'.

He died in 1931, before air transport needed to be added and before the London Passenger Transport Act 1933 made the concept of interdependence a reality. After York he had been a member of Westminster and then of Harpenden meeting. And *Modern transport* described him as a 'man whose views were independent and not always popular; a man who had the moral courage to express and uphold his opinions whatever the strength of the opposition which arrayed itself against him'.

As a boy in Whitby, Arnold E. Sewell (1886-1969) was taken to see a 94-year-old who, as a young man, had been a driver on the Stockton & Darlington in 1825. Sitting in a wooden armchair outside his door the old man told the boy tales of how locomotive-hauled trains and horse-drawn carriages had to jockey for priority on the same set of rails.

After Ackworth and Bootham AES commenced in 1903 as a clerk on the North Eastern at £25 pa: the rule was that all youths should start at £15 pa 'but I was given two years' seniority because it was thought that with an Ackworth education I was worth the extra £10'. He later

specialised on rates and charges for freight (on which he became an authority) and was LNER goods manager for Scotland.

In the late 1930s he was responsible for a joint road-rail committee to try to overcome pointless competition by sensible planning: this work continued through the war years 'until the politicians came in and the railways became the ball in a game of political ping-pong' (he could chide with kindly humour). The Transport Act 1947 limited the distance a public road haulier might normally carry freight to a radius of 25 miles from base 'but following a change of government the restriction was rescinded for political reasons, and with that went all hope of road and rail co-ordination, and the big, heavy, long distance lorries began to appear on the high roads'.

Following the 1947 Act AES (whose portrait is shown above) became charges adviser to the British Transport Commission and, shortly after, one of the three members of the Transport Tribunal, a body appointed by the Crown to control charges made by nationalised transport and a court of appeal as regards licences to operate held by road hauliers.

He retired in 1956, settling at Winscombe, Somerset, where he put his energies into the Sidcot Friends Housing Society, the sheltered accommodation known as Sewell House standing as a memorial to his labours.

After the second world war the railways found their physical assets depleted, strained to the utmost by the war effort. There had already been disinvestment before the war and clearly substantial finance was needed for modernisation. The only obvious source was the State. But the Transport Act 1947 did not bring with nationalisation the needed capital, for the government decided to concentrate early post-war investment in other sectors. And, though the Act provided for an integrated system of all inland transport, there was, perhaps, a simplistic assumption that nationalisation would bring this automatically.

Many provisions of the Act were barely in operation before the Transport Act 1953 reintroduced competition. Within a decade the Transport Act 1962 reversed the concept of integration by breaking the British Transport Commission into five autonomous transport bodies, the British Railways Board being given the financial task of breaking even as soon as possible.

During the 1950s a method of accountancy had developed by which total costs were (by methods considered by many to be crude) allocated to specific traffic. During Beeching's chairmanship of the British Transport Commission and British Railways Board (1961-5) these accounting criteria obtained, and his 1963 report, *The reshaping of British railways,* was based on the clear understanding that commercial principles were paramount.

After schooldays at Bootham, Robert A. Long (1917-1985), whose portrait is shown above, joined the London & North Eastern in 1935 as a traffic apprentice. His father, Robert J. Long, was well-known as secretary of the Northern Friends Peace Board 1914-43. After posts in the operating, finance and commercial departments, RAL became (1960) assistant general manager of BR's Scottish Region before becoming chief commercial manager for the British Transport Commission. At this time he was also chairman of the BR side of the Channel Tunnel Working Party. In 1967 he was appointed chief planning manager to the British Railways Board and in 1969 executive director (passenger services).

In January 1966 he with others wrote a paper urging 'a public service obligation' where the government would be invited to support non-commercial parts of the railway for social reasons. This approach found expression in the Transport Act 1968 where, for the first time, distinction was made between the commercial and non-commercial sectors. In 1970 Robert Long was urging that, for half the cost of getting Concorde into operation, a rational and coherent service could be provided for London's million and a quarter commuters, with decent travelling conditions: his prime concern was effective public transport.

In 1968 he chaired sessions of the International Railway Congress, Vienna, devoted to the economics of high speed passenger services. After a time as chief executive of BR International he retired in 1980, setting up his own transport consultancy. He wrote, with John Johnson, *British railway engineering, 1948-80* (1981), a record of the achievements of the engineering and research departments of BR during a time of vast change and innovation in railway technology, setting these developments within the wider framework of transport policy in Britain.

Robert Long and his family had settled in Beaconsfield in 1961 and for the last 24 years of his life he was a member of Jordans meeting.

A SCHOOLBOY EXPLOIT

In 1906 the North Eastern opened new offices in York – 'a huge palace of business'. In the 'Miscellany' column of the *Manchester Guardian* in March 1916 a strange episode there is recounted, though for security reasons with no mention of the place:

> The discovery of large letters painted in white on the roof of the building was reported by the astonished officials to the military authorities, and the opinion was arrived at that the letters might be a signal to raiding German aircraft.

> The inquiry led to the appearance of the headmaster of a most respectable school belonging to a body well known for their pacifist convictions. The schoolmaster explained to the astonished and incredulous commission that the white lettering was the work of a daredevil pupil of his blameless establishment!

> Both the military and the railway powers refused to believe that anyone could climb unaided to the high roof of the building, but the lad who had confessed to the feat came forward and offered to do the climb again.

> Needless to say his suggestion was not accepted, but his story had to be believed, for the letters were his own initials, and he was able to produce a witness who had been present when he did it during the dark hours of night. He had actually reached the roof by foot and hand hold on corner-stones not

more than an inch in width, and had returned in safety by the same perilous path. The whole escapade was the outcome of a schoolboy 'dare'.

The Bootham schoolboy was Oliver Ellis – 'a fearless football player, a brilliant and daring gymnast' wrote Arthur Rowntree, his headmaster. Ellis was a good naturalist (as witness his astute photographs of the hatching of a cuckoo's egg – another illicit early morning excursion from school). He had great imaginative and literary gifts – his school essay purporting to be from a soldier who had been through Gallipoli is still terrifyingly compelling. His great grandfather, Joseph Ellis, was brother to John, he of the Leicester & Swannington and the Midland.

He left Bootham in summer 1916 for the Royal Flying Corps. His exploits went ahead of him. On 21 April 1917 he wrote home: 'The [Friends Ambulance Unit] dentist I went to the other day said, "Let me see, you're the man who tried to whitewash the roof of some railway buildings in York, aren't you?"'.

A month later, on 20 May, Oliver Ellis was killed in action. His brother Colin lived to be a historian of Leicester; his brother Richard became an eminent pediatrician and undertook Quaker relief work in Spain; his sister Christine devoted her life to the community in which she lived, to Quaker education and, after the second world war, to relief work in the Netherlands.

CHARLES HOLDEN AND THE UNDERGROUND

Charles Holden (1875-1960) – no relation to James – was born near Bolton, Lancs, and after apprenticeship to a Manchester architect went to London as a young man. Among his early works was the Bristol Central Library (1906).

The establishment of the Design & Industries Association in 1915 brought together Holden (whose portrait is shown here), Frank Pick (then commercial manager of London Underground) and H. H. Peach of Dryad Handicrafts fame, an attender at Leicester Friends' meeting. Pick later involved Holden in the design of Underground stations: those on the Morden extension (1926) of what was later the Northern Line were in the stripped classical manner and faced with Portland stone. Then came the Underground headquarters building, 55 Broadway, above St James's Park station, completed in 1930. That year Pick and Holden toured Holland, Germany and Scandinavia: modern Dutch architecture strongly influenced Holden's designs for new stations in brick on the Piccadilly Line extensions (1931-3), notable being Arnos Grove, illustrated here.

Among Holden's later works are London University Senate House (1931-7), the National Library of Wales (1933) and Birkbeck College, the London University Students Union and the Warburg Institute (1952-8). He has been described in his professional career as 'a man of peculiar modesty who believed that architecture is a collective effort' and as 'one of the greatest architects of his generation and a designer who was anxious to use modern methods and a modern idiom without ever forgetting the lessons of tradition'.

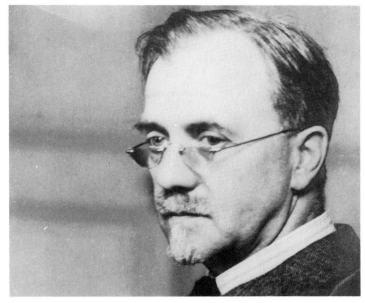

His wife, Margaret, had worked in the Friends War Victims Relief Committee's clothing warehouse during the first world war. Charles and Margaret Holden settled at Harmer Green, near Welwyn, where their home was always open to their friends, new and old, and anyone in difficulty was sure to seek his sensitive and wise advice. He spoke little, as though he distrusted speech, and only used the barest necessary. He was a great lover of music, playing the cello and later the piano. The Holdens were long years attenders of Hertford meeting, though never in fact joining Friends. And Charles was well content if meetings for worship were held wholly in silence.

THE SEVERN-LAMB WORKS

After schooldays at Ackworth, where he developed a love of all things mechanical, Peter Severn Lamb (1921-1975) travelled to the west coast of South America as a cleaner in the engine room of a tramp steamer and was then apprenticed to the engineering firm of Priestman Brothers at Hull, serving in various departments including the drawing office. While there he was asked to construct models of the firm's mechanical grabs. Two of the directors, Sydney H. Priestman and Philip Priestman, were grandsons to Samuel, whom we met on page 11 as a director of the North Eastern.

During the second world war Peter served as a pilot in RAF Coastal & Transport Command. On demobilisation he joined his parents who were starting an hotel at Stratford-on-Avon. He returned to model making, completing an LNER-type 0-6-0 in a workshop he created from a derelict garage at the back of the hotel and building a 7¼″ gauge railway in the garden.

A model of a cold steel pickling mill was exhibited at the 1949 British Industries Fair and a succession of orders decided Peter to create the firm of Severn-Lamb Ltd, Stratford-on-Avon. In 1960 came the first commission from the Smithsonian Institution, Washington, USA, which now has 38 Severn-Lamb models, including the Darby iron bridge at Coalbrookdale.

Besides model-making the firm has developed leisure transport, both water and rail. Peter was an active member of the Talyllyn Railway, Merioneth, and the

scale models by SEVERN-LAMB LTD.

firm began to produce passenger-hauling locomotives and coaches to the designs of David Curwin. Over 100 locomotives have been constructed, including the diesel hydraulic *Shelagh of Eskdale* on the Ravenglass & Eskdale.

Peter Lamb is shown here leaning out of the cab of the 0-6-0 'Dougal' tank engine, a type originally supplied for Longleat and available on 10¼″ & 15″ gauge.

Peter was a lover of mountains and moorland and before the end of his all-too-short life had completed his walk the length of the Pennine Way. He was a member of the small meeting at Ettington, south Warwickshire, whose 1678 meeting house was beloved also of John Betjeman.

FOOTPLATE &
SIGNAL BOX

My own time as a booking clerk on the Great Western was brief – and anyway we are, with one exception (see next page), avoiding the living. But who shall we choose?

There is Richard Baker (1844-1922) of Leominster, at one time on the Great Western as stoker and later engine driver (he would graphically describe the bursting of his locomotive's boiler) – a devoted adult school worker, a recorded minister, elder and overseer in his Quaker meeting, and a reprover of grumblers. Or John James (1854?-1946), who had been at William Knowles' school at The Pales, Radnorshire, and who was many years pointsman at Penybont and then signalman at Llandrindod Wells, where he was one of the founder members of the meeting in 1893 and where his Bible class was one of the features of the religious life of the town.

Or there is Joseph Clampitt (1871-1932) whose portrait is shown here. He was for some 30 years from 1895 a railwayman at York, and a tower of strength to the Leeman Road adult school and Friends' meeting (a meeting comprised largely of railway families). On moving to Kirkby Stephen about 1925 as locomotive

foreman he and Frank Parrott began holding meetings for worship in Friends' homes until in 1930 suitable premises were acquired.

Or John Scaife (1870-1925) who also came to Quakers through the adult schools in York, first at Old Priory and, after his marriage, at Burton Lane. He and his wife joined Friends in 1913 and he enjoyed showing Bootham boys round the railway sheds and recounting stories of his driving days. The strain of long hours of overtime during the war told on even his great strength and for the last years of his life he had to leave the footplate and undertake the lighter – but responsible and sometimes daunting – task of overlooker of the cleaning boys at the York sheds: he is shown among them on the right of this picture.

Finally, from so many fascinating characters, there is Titus Waddington (1811?-1877), the lame station master of Huttons Ambo, riding on a donkey to Malton meeting. Would that there were a picture of him doing so.

Let us give thanks for all those who have given us safe journeys.

'THAT MAZE OF LINES'

George Ottley (whose portriat is shown right) is the sole living person to find a place here, but this book would be incomplete were pride of place not given to his monumental *Bibliography of British railway history* (1965), with its near 8,000 entries. The second edition in 1983 was followed by a 1988 *Supplement*, making 12956 descriptions in all, arranged by subject and magnificently indexed.

George Ottley, a member of Friends Ambulance Unit in the second world war, was on the staff of the British Museum and University of Leicester libraries, a member of Petts Wood, Leicester and Rye meetings — and a lifelong practising church organist.

On completion of the bibliography he was presented with a sonnet, the octave running:

Ottley! Thy signal falls, the green lamp shines!
England had need of thee: too long no pen
Industrious essay'd the task, while men
Wander'd benighted in that maze of lines
Proliferate. Though now the rail declines
(By suspect interest hemm'd) and ne'er again
Such mighty splendours various meet our ken
Still in thy work stand forth the great designs.

'That maze of lines proliferate'. The maze of companies over nearly a century and three quarters is bewildering enough. The maze of publications by them or about them is more so. We must be ever thankful to the skill of George Ottley and others whose reference books are guides to us through that maze.

'Though now the rail declines'. During the 30 years 1961-90 route mileage has shrunk from 17,830 to 10,307 and stations open to passengers from 7,000 to 2,483. Some, perhaps much, of this might have made sense had it been planned as part of a co-ordinated and efficient system of public transport where remunerative services supported those that were necessary but unremunerative. Alas, it was not so.

The excursionists in this pen and ink drawing ('the world's people' rather than Quakers by their dress) are about to benefit from the interdependence of various forms of transport, for John Joseph Wilson (1836-1903), Bootham scholar and Leeds Quaker leather manufacturer, entitled his sketch 'A steam-tug excursion: the start'. As for us, we are near the end of our excursion, our journey through this book. For want of time we have missed many people of interest, even of importance (not a mention, for instance, of the Quaker engineers on the Bristol & Exeter). But J. J. Wilson's drawing not only reminds us that public transport is all about people. It reminds us, too, that though we are at the end of this book's journey, there are many other excursions awaiting us.

ENVOI

James Tangye (1826?–1913), the engineer and successful businessman, the creator with his brother of the world-famous Cornwall Works in Birmingham, had in retirement returned to his native Cornwall, living simply, still the modest if obsessionally thorough workman.

A friend described his workshop as 'in a very real sense his spiritual home; for here in his little engineering paradise the best life of his later years was lived, and here was carried on, in his own never-failing patient way, the search for truth'.

He was a godsend to neighbours with vacillating clocks or broken tea kettles and he used his workshop to encourage and enable fisher lads to become engineers. And after work he would spend quiet moments in his observatory with its 4-inch equatorial telescope. He was well past 80 before the time came to set his tools on one side.

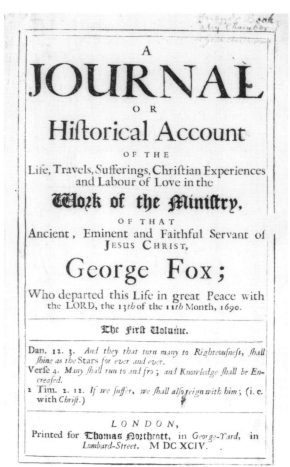

His friend William Bellows wrote: 'He dearly loved every form of time-keeping apparatus; but I think his chief "mechanical love" was the locomotive. He never tired of it nor of listening to the story of a railway-journey; and he would drive for miles to catch a glimpse of an express train. Only last month, as he lay nearing the end, he was heard to say in a quiet voice, "I *love* trains"; with so much earnestness and meaning put into that word *love*.'

In his observatory he loved to read and to meditate. He loved especially the record of the early Friends, prizing them because they testified to the Universal Light in which he himself believed. A neighbouring Quaker would drop in of an evening and find the octogenarian James Tangye reading George Fox's *Journal* – 'He was a good, dear man', he would say, 'and I never tire of reading his *Journal*'.

ACKNOWLEDGMENTS

ooking at ways in which to commemorate in 1991 the tercentenary of the death of George Fox, a group of Friends known as the Bunhill Fields Group hoped, amongst other things, to persuade British Rail to name a locomotive after him, an ecumenical companion to BR's *John Wesley*. That proposal, alas, did not prosper but the group persevered with its suggestion that there should also be a booklet on Quakers and railways and invited me to undertake it. My first thanks, therefore, go to the Bunhill Fields Group and, in particular, to Elsa Dicks and Farrand Radley. Allied to these thanks is my gratitude, and the group's, to the Bedford Institute Association for its help with the administrative backup.

Preparation has been possible through generous help from the Joseph Rowntree Charitable Trust and publication through the Sessions Book Trust and other trusts that wish to remain anonymous: without their practical support the idea would have remained an idea. All concerned are profoundly grateful for their help.

I wish to thank everyone at the Ebor Press for all they have done in producing the book – and, in particular, Bryan Blackwell for his design. Beyond these general thanks I would like to record particular gratitude to William and Margot Sessions whose frequent hospitality and continuing lively interest have been heartwarming.

The resources of many libraries have enormously helped me, and if I mention but two – Friends House Library, London, and the National Railway Museum, York – it is not that I have forgotten the many others but just that I used them less often. The same goes for books. I had thought to mention the half dozen I have leaned on most frequently but I found that, as I said to myself, 'If A, why not B?', the list grew to impossible size. I therefore forbear to mention any, trusting that, in a necessarily unfootnoted book, anyone tempted to mutter 'He got that from my book' will generously accept a heartfelt if silent acknowledgement. A typescript *Sources and references* will be available at the Library of the Society of Friends, London.

The locomotive shown on the front cover is a T. W. Worsdell design (see pages 30 and 31): I am most grateful to Peter Van Zeller for his kind response to my *cri de coeur*. The copyright is his.

The back cover includes a reproduction of the 'Quakers and the early railways' panel of the Quaker Tapestry: besides a number of Quakers the panel depicts George Stephenson (1781-1848) and John Wilkinson (1728-1808) so as to avoid any undue parochialism; copyright is acknowledged to the Quaker Tapestry Scheme. The initial L to these acknowledgments is from *Bradshaw's descriptive guide to the Great Western Railway* (1845).

Most of the illustrations are from Friends House Library to whom enquiry should be made in relation to copyright. In the following cases copyright rests elsewhere: National Railway Museum (pp. 7 left, 9 left, 11 lower, 12, 20, 25 lower, 30, 31 top two); North Woolwich Old Station Museum (pp. 28 lower, 29 all three); London Transport Museum (p. 35); Boothan School (p. 34 upper); C. & J. Clark, Street (p. 23 both); Severn-Lamb Ltd (p. 36 both); Maude Clampitt (p. 37 upper); William Harris (pp. 21, 40, tickets); Muriel Long (p. 33 right); Michael Metford-Sewell (p. 33 left); George Ottley (p. 38 upper); Ruth Pashley (pp. 24 both, 25 upper, 32); Christopher Scaife (p. 37 lower); John Tindale (page 31 lower); the author (p. 1 both). I apologise to anyone whose copyright I may unwittingly have infringed.

Any book however modest (as this is) depends on correspondence and conversations with a whole host of people. Besides those already mentioned I would like to say a general 'Thank you' to many unnamed and a special 'Thank you' to W. V. Awdry, Lyn Brooks, Sylvia Carlyle, Ann Chase, Richard Clark, Michael Farr, Michael Lamb, Muriel Long, Michael Metford-Sewell, Mary Milligan, Hugh Murray, George Ottley, James Priestman, Henry Rowntree, Jack Simmons, Margaret Simpson, Malcolm Thomas, Terry Turbin, Gerard Wakeman. None of them, needless to say, is responsible for any inadequacies, inaccuracies or infelicities that remain. Nor is John Lamont, but for whose steady cheerful encouragement the whole enterprise might have come to a grinding halt as a result of the wrong kind of snow or of leaves on the line.

Edward H. Milligan
April 1992